dandelion

Also by Heather Swan

Poetry
A Kinship with Ash

The Edge of Damage (chapbook)

Prose
*Where the Grass Still Sings: Stories of Insects
and Interconnection*

Where Honeybees Thrive: Stories from the Field

dandelion

Heather Swan

Terrapin Books

Terrapin Books
4 Midvale Avenue
West Caldwell, NJ 07006

www.terrapinbooks.com

ISBN: 978-1-947896-69-7
Library of Congress Control Number: 2023942424

First Edition

Cover art by Heather Swan
Light Beings from Ancestor Series
mixed media on board, 12" x 9.5"

for Maia and Elijah,
with so many wishes

Contents

. . . the knowing animals are aware
that we are not really at home in our interpreted world.

—Rainer Maria Rilke

Invitation

At the forest's cusp
      a sacred pull

from leaf mold,
      xylem, phloem,

blood of the sparrow,
      blood of the shrew,

all of us of a kind.
      There is an invitation,

beyond the noise
      of industry and ego,

a veil you and I
      can slip through.

While the World Burned On

for Lailah

The geese shot across the water
like a squadron, a line of them,
two feet above the surface. We were
caught in their path, my canoe
merely a shape cut out
of the gathering gray light of dusk.
We watched them coming
between lake and sky, mirror images
of their bodies just below them
as they grew larger and larger,
unwavering, passing us close enough
that the sound of their wings
pressing against the wind
left us gasping, awakened
from the spell you had cast
with your words moments before
about your dead son—
that had us floating only
on the cavernous grief,
his bones silting in the spring,
your empty hands, my own dead
returning, while the hole
left by the virus widened
beneath us like the dark water,
and the palimpsest
of the many violences
was suddenly so clear, and
we were descending.
We were out of time, meaning,
not in it, but then a breath later,

the moonlight flickered
on the surface of the water and
that sound of wings, and we were back
in the boat, the geese pulling us forward
as they did the impossible—
not stopping, but flying on together,
though the air was thick with dread
and there was so very little light.

Dumbo

Since 1986, the Asian elephant has been listed as Endangered on the IUCN Red List, as the population has declined by at least 50 percent over the last three elephant generations.

The pile of severed elephant tusks
in the black and white photograph
reaches higher than the heads of the men
standing proudly on each side. I did not
count how many dead it meant. Once,
in the heat of the Terai, an elephant
took me home. We rocked together
with each of her steps, my legs bent
behind her ears. Other elephants
passed us by, some carrying lumber,
others a harvest, still others ambling
unencumbered along the village road.
What a surprise, the warm breath in my hand
as she nuzzled it with the end of her trunk.
So much I didn't know then. They say
elephants remember their comrades
even after years of separation,
that they communicate over miles
with sounds inaudible to human ears, that
when they see a family member killed
they suffer inside like us.
Remember Dumbo's feather,
my mother used to say, meaning,
we are capable of more than we know.

Summons

The barred owls drew me
                into the trees

the way death withdrew him
                from this world.

I tried to read
                the moonlit calligraphy,

tree branches tracing
                the veins to my heart.

With my palms flat
                on the trunk of the elm

I closed my eyes. It was then
                I saw the forest fires,

saw the flames licking,
                saw whole hillsides

crackling, saw the pain
                was not unlike mine.

After *The Last Glacier*

—an exhibit of images by Todd Anderson and Bruce Crownover

the movement   where there should be none

the unsettling of ice   soil   stone

green   where it doesn't belong

the ice leaving   like a beloved disappearing

before your eyes

unwell withering

cheeks and limbs thinning   hollows deepening

bones no longer a mystery

what disappears   into a vastness

which is the sea

an unknown

which is the sea

we have made

the adulterated sea

moving water   that can't be quelled

in this warm air

like all that leaks   a shattered cup

no use trying to hold

what can't be held in

the inevitable spread

of spilled milk, no use

crying now

here the diminished

once a blanket   now tatters of snow

        patches   of gray white
    where a white bear
                        might have walked
    where a white owl
                        might have watched
    where a white hare—

here the lack
                        of forethought, of conscience
        and what remains   is the silt
                            of regret   no penance

    is equal to   the damage   we have left

soon the bare future
                bare drumlin   bare kettle   bare moraine

Field Notes: Human Being

Observe now, homo sapiens:
hot-blooded, bipedal, equipped
with tricky opposable thumbs and brains
much bigger than their hearts.
Omnivorous and always hungry,
they consume, consume, consume.
A species much like a volcano—
always spilling beyond themselves,
leaving nothing but ash in their wake.
Evolved to preserve their fantasies,
rather than life itself. Evolved
to be entertained. See how
they eliminated the source
of their lives, how they cut
down the trees, their own breath,
how they poisoned the waters,
the blood in their veins, destroyed
the earth, what fed their flesh.
And oh, how they loved
their plastic and their guns.
They held stones in their palms at the end,
stolen minerals polished smooth for shine:
yellow jasper for tenacity,
red-banded agate for endurance and calm.
They who brought this apocalypse on.
They who invented racing.
They who invented a game called roulette,
and who loved to watch movies
that stoked their pulse.

Now as the earth rescinds its offerings,
they cluster together in the urban quiet,
clutching amethyst, the promise of healing,
and cool green prehnite for peace.

Redress for Michelangelo

In 1559, during Michelangelo's lifetime, Paul IV employed
Daniele da Volterra to paint loincloths on the nudes in the
Sistine Chapel.

Imagine climbing into that ceiling,
into all that color and light
in order to mask that masterpiece,

the beauty somehow despised,
the way we've learned to despise the gold
in a field of dandelions.

As if seeing our own bodies
might damage us
like staring too long at the sun.

Imagine obscuring the work of a man
whose renderings came from years of attention
to lips, shoulders, thighs,

who, in a room somewhere,
was still fumbling with his charcoal
toward perfect chiaroscuro.

History

your body is a smooth body
your body is a desert drilled for petroleum
your body is a trout stream drying
your body is a splinter pulled from the tree
your body is a ferris wheel at the carnival spinning
you may not recognize this body
you did not remain silent, but still
your body is a jet plane carrying other bodies
your body is spent jet fuel
you may not understand the words
your body is an old story, your body is a tweet
your body is an orchard, a tendril, a ripened plum falling
your body is a wound
you may not remember the blades or the blasts
your body is an astral body, a celestial body
a body barely understood as body
but it is the only body you have
and it holds your honeyed secrets and it holds your lead
body of air, body of atoms, body of light

Why Not Mercy

During the Crusades,
upon learning his enemy,
Richard the Lionheart, was ill,
Saladin sent him peaches and snow.
Not in surrender, but in chivalry.
A small kindness in the midst of war.
How can these coexist?
Watch how we pour tea
as the building is bombed.
How the finger sandwiches. The cups.
How the cold peaches, dripping
their sweet. How the paper
is signed. The button pushed.
How the man who ate peaches still
slaughtered. How there were countless
women and children and men.
How nothing changes.
And how nothing stays—does it?—
but politics and war.
How much can we feel?
How much is too much?
How dead are we already?
How the song in our earphones.
How the bolted door.
How there are no more beds.
How the bullets, the smoke.
How this quilt is the only one left.

Mortal

How impossible to forget
in that late equatorial light
on one lonely edge of the Pacific,
those thousands of crabs
no bigger than thumbnails
who scurried away from our feet
as we walked across the sand,
each step setting off a ripple,
a tide of tiny creatures
so afraid of us, even though we
had no intention to harm,
and how you sought
the sense of humility
the ocean provides, sought
to surrender your worn,
human self, and so let
the dark waves take and toss you
among the fists of gneiss
as I stood frozen on the beach,
the magnificent frigatebirds
ushering you home.

Field Notes: Crow

Today the crows
        came like a posse,

cloaked, and crowding
        into the pine pillars

by my house, cawing
        their allegations

against us as the earth
        continues to burn.

I want to transcribe
        the language

of their ink black
        silhouettes, knowing

it's only a dream
        I harbor,

that they assemble to scold
        the human race.

Could it be
        they blame us

for everything,
        which we deserve?

But they plot and pursue
        their corvid schemes,

clean the carrion
           from the road,

ignore my useless apologies,
           and continue

to bring trinkets
           to the children.

Wile E. Coyote

The Coyote teaches how wisdom and folly go together. In others'
mistakes we see our own foolishness and can learn from their mistakes.
—Shamanic Journey

In the middle of the desert
between two cliffs steepling up
on either side of a road, sits
the bowl of "Free Bird Seed"
to lure the purple blur of roadrunner
to stop and eat long enough
for Wile E. Coyote—master of
technology, who is perched
on one cliff edge, hands on a zipline
strung between the two walls of rock—
to swoop down and snatch her up.

Soon enough, Roadrunner
charges into the scene, stops
for a quick snack, and narrowly
escapes capture . . . *Meep Meep* . . .
as Coyote flies down
on his nefarious contraption
and finding no purchase
and no way to slow down
slams into the other wall
and crumples. The next day
he will return with dynamite.

Ritual for the New Ancestors

As the moon wanes, watch
        for the raft of coots

floating on the water
        too frigid to swim in,

small bodies clustered
        close together the way

we humans might gather
        in our grief when

it is possible to gather.
        Let the strong wind

pass through you—
        have you seen the wind

comb a field of bluestem?—
        and wait to feel something

untangle, your sharpnesses
        suddenly smoothing. An owl

will call out above your head;
        let it fill your hollows.

There will be stars
        caught in the water;

let your dark eyes
        mirror that shine.

A white stag will appear
        at the edge of a wood,

and you will know again
        your own heart.

What I tell you
        is not a fairy tale.

II

Metaphor

Beneath the maple, the child lifts
her hands and becomes gossamer
while a stream of air comes through her lips.

"Breeze," someone says.

Then her fingers press
a green flatness with ridges
first to her palm, then to her cheek.

"Leaf," someone says.

Above, watch as the trees articulate wind,
allowing it wholly in,
and how birds so easily navigate
the chaos of branch and leaf.

How unequipped we are,
intent on naming things,
making maps. And how small
our window, how very small.

But look, the child
has discovered a nectarine
in a bowl by the open door,
and through its sweetness
spills glossolalia.

A Story Which Borrows Its Section Titles from Albums by The Cure

I. The Top

In the year 2008, scientists said devastation was on the horizon.
That there was no stopping it.
That we'd begun the downward slide.

II. Staring at the Sea

And look, an elaborate castle made entirely of sand.

III. Boys Don't Cry

In the stories the storyteller tells, loss
after loss is wrapped in music
and gold light.

IV. Japanese Whispers

Her smile when she returns
        from her father's house
is a Japanese screen—
           its elegant asymmetry carefully designed
             to distract the viewer
               from anything that lies
      behind it.

V. Kiss Me Kiss Me Kiss Me

Once there was a hummingbird
who flew into my house
and then couldn't find his way out again.
He flew over and over into the glass,
the unsteady whir of his wings like a car
revving to free itself from snow.
I caught him behind the curtain
when he was vulnerable and imprecise
and folded my fingers around him,
his shivering heart. Outside, he stretched
his luminous wings, blinked twice, and
in a blur was gone.

VI. Wish

Her finger
paintings not
washed away
by rain.

VII. Freakshow

In the car from the back seat the little boy asks, Who stays in that
jail? The people who made bad choices, says the mother. Like
what? he asks. Like driving drunk or fistfighting, she says, but don't
worry, Love, the really bad guys go to prison. What's prison? he
asks. Oh, she tells him, it's far away, and there are police guarding
it all the time. The whole place is surrounded with huge walls and
barbed wire. There's no way they can get out of there. And then
she can hear that he's crying. What is it? she says. And his voice is
very small. But do they ever get to go outside? Do they ever get to
see their mums? And what if they're really sorry? Mum, we don't
even treat animals that way.

VIII. The Only One

So many things that simply never turned out right.

IX. Faith

If I plant them, my father tells me,
the seeds he collected from his hollyhocks
will bloom in two years time.

X. Happily Ever After

In the papers, there are pictures of the melting,
the ice caps breaking apart,
and it's clear, we must learn
how to walk here.

XI. In Between Days

Tonight, the fireflies write on the air in a language we
        can't understand.
And from the drawer a letter written in his hand.

XII. Galore

Nothing left to say but,
thank you.

Thank you.

Piglet

28 billion pounds of pork is produced in the U.S. each year.
—Kevin Shutz, *Farm Progress*, 2022

Oh tender ear, oh Piglet,
oh kindest friend of Pooh.
Oh pig. Oh soft snout
snuffling succulent soil,
oh voluptuous flanks
flouncing about, fed to fill out
for the plates of men. Bacon
is not a word we used when
visiting our neighbor's barn,
flitting past stalls where you lay
whispering to your young,
their eyes barely open,
so drowsy with warmth
and drink. We know now
how smart you are, how
you ache like we do. And still
we, with our bellies full,
read the bedtime stories:
Somewhere near
One Hundred Acre Wood
past Christopher Robin's house,
the Piglet was sitting
on the ground . . . blowing
happily at a dandelion.

Crop Duster

I.

At dawn, an airplane roars over
the rooftop, close enough
to shake the windows,
close enough to wake her,
and a rattle is set loose
in her body. Adrenalin
raises her head, and she listens.
The whine of the engine
trails off, but then arcs,
accelerates, grows louder.
Grabbing her baby girl,
she races downstairs.
Is the pilot suicidal?
She opens the door,
steps outside, her child
flattened to her chest.
The sound deafens now
as the airplane sheers
the tips of the pines,
bearing down again
on her home. Not until
it is shrinking away
does she feel the mist
settling on her skin.
Wanting to wretch,
she reels back in,
rushes to find faucets
for rinsing.

II.
"Residents: Spraying will begin in early May, weather dependent. Trained pilots will treat approximately 1,235 acres in 8 counties as part of the 2007 gypsy moth suppression program . . . Some people with severe allergies may wish to avoid areas to be sprayed on the day that spraying occurs."

III.
A lump in the little
girl's neck swells
to the size of a mango.
She is too young
to be afraid. Doctors
take measurements
and needle her arms,
but find no solid answer.
Does she have allergies? Yes.
Has she suffered from asthma? Yes.
The mother mentions the plane
and the mist *just 2 weeks before.*
And the neighbors sprayed
their lawns then, too.
There is no evidence
chemicals were the cause.
Surgery is the solution.
If the gland does not go down,
we'll cut it out.
But there is no way to prove
the root cause.

IV.
"Recognizing Pesticide Poisoning: Mild poisoning or early symptoms of acute poisoning: headache, fatigue, weakness, dizziness, restlessness, nervousness, perspiration, nausea, diarrhea,

loss of appetite, loss of weight, thirst, moodiness, soreness in joints, skin irritation and irritation of eyes, nose and throat. Moderate poisoning ... excessive saliva, stomach cramps, excessive perspiration, trembling, no muscle coordination, muscle twitches, extreme weakness, mental confusion, blurred vision, difficulty in breathing, coughing, rapid pulse, flushed or yellow skin and uncontrollable crying. Severe or acute poisoning ... fever, intense thirst, increased rate of breathing, vomiting, uncontrollable muscle twitches, pinpoint pupils, convulsions, inability to breathe and unconsciousness ... Chronic poisoning occurs as the result of repeated, small, non-lethal doses through a longer period of time ... Symptoms such as nervousness, slowed reflexes, irritability or a general decline of health."

—Oklahoma Cooperative Extension Service

V.

Gypsy moth
caterpillars
die as quickly
as those of all
the other butterflies
and moths
in the range
of fumigation.

VI.

In the faded photo,
the two tiny girl children,
grin in the sunlight,
chins glistening with
juice, the paler one
holding a peach

by her cheek.
Like a measuring stick
for her lymph gland.

VII.
". . . Currently, 300 million pounds of glyphosate are applied each
year to American farms . . . In general, chemical companies can
claim "safe" equals "not toxic," meaning it won't kill a human in 96
hours . . . . Regardless . . . hundreds of studies have recently shown
a wide variety of harm from glyphosate-based herbicides,
including neurotoxicity, liver disease, thyroid disorders, endocrine
disruption, birth defects, testes and sperm damage, growth of
breast cancer cells, increased non Hodgkin's Lymphoma, the
destruction of gut bacteria which leads to numerous autoimmune
diseases and autism symptoms, and more."
—*The Hill*, March 17, 2017

VIII.
At twelve, the girl
is taller than her mother.
Friends tease her
about the scar on her neck
which looks to them
like a love bite. This spring,
her white blood cells surged,
her feet turned blue,
her temperature spiked
and spiked again.
Tremors rocked
her body. Plus nosebleeds.
Lethargy. Vomiting.
The doctors tested her
for autoimmune disorders.
No connection,

her mother reassured
herself when her daughter
was stable again. Mornings
she does what she can:
organic oranges,
organic eggs,
organic bread.

Field Notes: Red Tail

The shadow
arrives first
by your feet,
then the whoosh
of her wide wings,
like a storm front
consuming sky,
feather and claw close enough
to brush your flesh.
She lands on
a jagged finger
of the ancient oak,
her eyes searing
into you,
a warning.

Bambi

A cool gray envelope of car light
holds us against the frigid dark while
the still-warm body of the mother deer
lies on gravel and shattered glass,
her white belly illuminated like a moon.
No cars pass. My son and I hover
above her, both of us knowing well
the ice blade of loss, the dangerous
vertigo of regret. Her baby had flown
through the air, so lithe in the fields,
now a crumpled flower. We kneel
to something, unbidden.
In the movie, Bambi gets to live.
Our voices, shards in our throats.
Once, in a field of goldenrod and aster,
a curious doe walked up to me,
her eyes never leaving my eyes,
ears quivering, nose tracing my scent.
Suspicious, but finding nothing to fear,
she came to me through the flowers,
a gaze that bore into my heart. If only
I could believe what she saw there.

Kermit

Because I'm not giving up . . .
　　　　—Kermit the Frog, *The Muppet Movie*

That morning, when you returned
from your tunnel of darkness,
the grasses of the marsh still brown
in early spring, the air
remembering the dead
of winter but offering
a promise of green,
a flicker of movement
pulled you from your hood
of despair, off the trail
and into the mud,
following the instinct you had
as a boy, something stronger
than the undertow, at last,
and your arm shot down
into the muck. You emerged
from the damp reeds cupping a tiny
frog, and I saw in your eyes
that spark, a gleam, inchoate,
as you stood again in your church
of cattails, and I believed then
you would survive.

Pastime

We drink dark coffee
while the leaf shadows
write in calligraphy
on the curtains.
Light keeps spilling like time
imperceptibly changing.
The plants drink it in,
and sometimes flower,
as we age and age.
The children grow tall
and take their paths, blossom.

Oh, how we wasted our days
with the senseless worries
and angers. How we overlooked
the importance of warm mugs,
the shift of light,
eyes that glanced back
to meet ours
as the children ran
out the front door.

Seventeen

Oh child, I remember
the tug of your shoelaces
across the tops
of your tiny shoes
and the careful
bows I made
to keep you safe
before you ran off
through the field
of dandelions, their
delicate seeds aloft
in clouds behind you,
rising with a thousand
wishes in the limitless
autumn-blue air.

In Which the Woman Avoids Transitions

Night rehearses the ending.

Winter expands its edges each day

even as flowers pry their way

out of the frozen soil. I crawl

back into bed after the birds

carve tunnels through our silence.

The children do not fit into

the clothing I have made them.

Once, the days were strawberries.

The dog sighs and shifts position.

No voice calls like a bell for me

lately. At dusk, the planets align.

Parkinson's

That which is known
so quickly can be shattered.
A splinter of insight,
and the certain is cracked open,
leaving behind it something
as amorphous as light.

The way the words of Copernicus
yanked the earth from stasis,
and thrust it into rotation,
sent it spinning wildly
into the black.

Or how when I learned
about my father's illness,
my world tipped
like a table set for dinner
which is suddenly lifted from one end—
everything sliding.
Panic sets in,
the scramble to catch
what is not yet broken,
then the search for a place
that seems solid
where you can sit down, hold
your favorite teacup
in your hands.

Synapse

In the canned fruit aisle of Walmart,
he reaches for apricots the way
one might reach for a robin's egg,
with a slowness akin to reverence.
His gait does not fail him today,
and I can almost pretend there's
no Parkinson's. It's work, though,
he says. He has to tell his knee to bend
and when. Tell his arm to reach.
The disease steals the art
of the synapse, steals the body
a bit at a time. His paintings
never mourned. One winter in
Wisconsin, after months of gray days,
his studio blossomed in canvases
covered with colors we had all forgotten.
Still he dreams of painting.
In frozen foods, he chooses
chicken stir-fry, cherry pie, pasty.
One day he called me early
in the morning, shocked to learn
he could crack an egg. Mornings
he still has his hands. Lately his voice
has been tissue-paper thin, so every word
has weight. Back at his studio
where he has chosen to live, I help
him carry the groceries inside. Today
when I leave, he gives me a painting
he knows I've loved—the red one

with the handprint hidden amid
birdwings. *Birds,* he tells me.
Caught in the updraft. Rising.

Field Notes: Polar Bear

The eye of the white bear punctures
        the landscape   of white
   like a porthole to a vast blackness
        an archaic knowing   an encryption.
His body lumbers forth   ghostlike
   over what is still frozen
        but is becoming water   rivulets
   carving the ice   like so many tears.
When he closes his eyes
        he'll disappear.

Silence

Not in the Zendo—
shifting robes, dripping eaves,
nor the desert—
wind rattling sagebrush, wind sweeping sand.
Not at the pond's edge in winter—
the whispering of cattails, the lonely tick of ice,
nor in the tallgrass prairie at dusk—
the circle of crickets, the grasshoppers' thrum.
Not in the second floor apartment at midnight—
the occasional car, the refrigerator's drone.

I've known no silence,
but in the small room
where my father died,
between his last breath
and the wail that rose
from deep inside my body.

On the Day After You Left This World

I floated out to the island
of bird bones, where
their long gone voices
now whisper in the cattails
looking for solitude, solace,
but found instead
three cranes waiting
who let me join them
there on the shore.
Night fell and we stayed, all of us,
cranes, crickets, cattails,
my broken body breathing,
and in the graying light
the breeze stroked
the cool waters of the lake,
the water lapping the soil
until all of it
was not separate, all of it
became one breath.

Field Notes: Cedar Waxwing

The weight of his limp
feathered body in my palm
was less than that of a lemon.
Still warm, his wild heart
beat against me—a waxwing
who believed the blue
of the shop window
to be more open sky.

I know the way what
looks to be a clear path
is often an illusion. Why is it
we only begin to trust
when we are truly broken?

Inside my house, he soon
stood, clutched my finger,
ate millet from my hand.
Within days, he flew
out of my life.

The Birds Are Just Birds
You Would Have Said

I'm always running from narrative.
  —My father, the painter Arthur Kdav (1944-2020)

Twenty-three days after your death,
                two of us took my canoe out at dawn,
        the mist softening everything,
                rising the way steam would rise
        from your cup of morning coffee,
                obscuring any obvious distinctions,
        which, I know, you would have liked,
                color and shape for their own sake.

Bird chatter broke night's quiet
                as tangerine light slowly stained the world.
        Our paddles dipped into the lake
                sending parentheses of purple, blue,
        peach, and gold across the glassy surface,
                as brilliant as one of your paintings.

In one of your last, you painted
                one black bird in flight,
        then painted it out, days later.
                Too obvious, maybe,
        for your abstract expressionist eye.

Near the edge of the marsh,
                we lit some incense and a candle,
        and eleven geese,
                like witnesses, gathered
        not far from the boat.

My friend began to chant
   the Daihishin Dharani,
  the soft rhythm of her voice,
    easy as the smoke which floated up
  in a brushstroke and disappeared into the sky.

All the while, the birds remained still,
    not moving even at the end
  of our prayer. But then after, as if on cue,
    the geese rose up, one by one
  like a string of electric lights,
    each lifting the next
  up off the water.

They looped toward the north
    with steady wingbeats,
  but circled back over us
    before following each other
  into the golden distance, the artist's
    vanishing point,
  and I knew, then, you were free.

The Arrival

In the dream, the animals arrive
at the door of my house, a mess of claws,

beaks and fur, hungry and so very thin.
The tiger—all teeth and sad eyes, head

as big as the space my circled arms make
when I pull someone closer to my

heart—soon pushes in. Fear is a tight-
fitting glove I pull off slowly, finger

by finger as he noses my daughter's face.
What stills me—what sinks me—

is the absence of malice and the abyss
of extinction balanced in his gaze.

I know they will always be arriving,
and the many ways we will say:

There's no more room at the inn.

IV

The Words of Noah's Wife: Day 1

The rain begins.
Inside the pitch
walls we breathe
quietly, animals
and humans,
exhausted from the labor
of preparation,
waiting. The sound
of the rain is a comb
which untangles
any knots remaining,
and we slip into sleep
until the ark shifts,
finally lifting
leaving a world,
heaving us into
an ending.

The Words of Noah's Wife: Day 5

With a candle I go
to feed the birds.
Today a sparrow flew
to me and landed
on my forearm.
Her tiny feet, like
the hands of a feverish child,
gripped my skin
as she drew near the flame.
I saw quickly she believed
the bit of light to be
a way back to the world
she knew—of trees, of branches,
the corridors of leaves,
the fluttering walls which
at anytime she chose
she could pass through,
then dive into deep blue.
I could not tell her,
there are no more trees.
She blinked in confusion
at the heat of the candle,
and eventually resignation
settled over her body
like muslin.
I carried her
back to her mate.

The Words of Noah's Wife: Day 7

In my dreams, I see
chairs rising and tipping
in the water, wooden spoons
floating and ridiculous, then
the empty dress of a child fills
for a moment, with air,
as smooth and round
as a mother's belly
before it twists in an eddy
and disappears. At least
the storm is deafening,
but even the wind wails.
As children we teased the waves—
the ocean's lapping tongue—
squealing when it licked our toes
or standing defiant as
beneath our feet
it sucked the sand
and pebbles away.

The Words of Noah's Wife: Day 10

There are seeds
in the hems
of my dresses
which I gathered
before the rain.
I opened each seam
and filled each furrow
with thick rows
of promise.
I feel them now
brushing my ankles:
melon, amaranth, almond,
thistle, cypress, lime.
Are they aware
of their potential?
Does the tomato seed
know of its kinship
with blood?

The Words of Noah's Wife: Day 13

By now, fish are flying
over mountains, circling
the crowns of alpine flowers.
Up here in the darkness
in a place without edges,
when the weeping begins,
the source is uncertain.
At first, it seems to come
from my children, perhaps
my daughter-in-law, or
is it an animal dreaming?
Soon I realize
the sound is married
to the ache in my own
body. Whose cry is this
that shakes my shoulders?
What is a river
out of its banks,
but water?

The Words of Noah's Wife: Day 17

From the window today,
I saw the world:
ash, the water,
ash, the sky.
The horizon line
has disappeared
like a line of charcoal
brushed away by a hand.
All day, I tried
to remember yellow:
wild mustard,
dandelion, daffodil—
just one daffodil
glowing like an ember
against the winter soil.
I know there must be
a yellow place
hidden deep in my body.
And to think there were
days in that house
when whole hillsides
went unnoticed.

The Words of Noah's Wife: Day 21

The smell of fresh dung
mingles with the sweet breath
of the gentle beasts. The yaks
sleep close to me. I found
some forgotten basil
folded into cloth;
the freshness lingers
on my hands. We measure
our days with the tasks
of feeding ourselves,
feeding the creatures,
and carrying our waste
to the upper deck
where we empty it
into the sea.

The Words of Noah's Wife: Day 23

The man
whose children
I carried
comes to me
in the night.
He shudders
on my breast
like a cottonwood
in the wind.
Our withered bodies,
once as supple
as the leopards
sleeping nearby,
rock slowly
without words
in the arms
of the ocean.

The Words of Noah's Wife: Day 28

The dusty wings
of the moths are fraying,
their fragile veins exposed
like roots exposed by winds
in a dry season.
They are so determined
to destroy themselves,
dizzily flirting
with flames.
Only now do I
understand them;
I've seen madness
open a door and
invite me
to step through.
How much damage
can we sustain?
How long will
the bees survive
without nectar?

The Words of Noah's Wife: Day 31

Dear sweet Mother,
I've remembered
your face, floating
above your loom
as we sat spinning
nearby. Today
I laid my hand
on the head
of a lion.
His forehead was
warm like mine.
He had no interest
in me. If this is not
the end of our world,
I will teach the children
the secret to keeping
the right tension between
warp and weft.
I will sing to them.
I will teach them
about seeds,
about sharing—
if there is a place
for us, mother,
I will.

The Words of Noah's Wife: Day 38

He's let the white bird
go. The black one
returned, its small
exhausted body
unwilling to fly again.
He believes
the words he heard.
I confess I did not
when he began
the felling,
the dragging
of all the great trees,
the building
of this ark.
I could not.
But I have risen
and fed all of us
each day.
We will wait.

The Words of Noah's Wife: Day 47

Oh sun, oh happy light!
Oh green! The sound
of no rain. The animals
still breathing.
And in the mouth
of the dove, the tiny branch
of an olive. A second chance.
I am breaking open, at last,
a lilac in April.

V

Field Notes: Muskrat

The ice begins
to take the lake
like skin over a wound,
the liquid becoming roof,
becoming floor to all
those who live here:
bipedal, winged, finned.
A muskrat moves
between the worlds
above and below the surface,
emerging and disappearing
again, like Persephone
was said to do. Oh,
how I want that fluidity—
to move so comfortably
between the unknown
and the known.

Prayer Wheel

A verticil of sepals,
        a velvet lavender whorl, soft
                as a pigeon's breast
      where the bee rests;
                this is my dreamscape.

Earth, hold me tenderly
        as a milkweed husk
                holds her seeds, as the tendrils
        of wild grapevine hold
                their droplets of dew,
        or the trembling fescue
                holds, for an instant, each
                        subtle breeze.

Carry me, please,
        back to the soil
                because I am caught
        in a current of exhaust
                from a city bent
                      on breaking
each of us, another copse
        turned to corpses, another field drowned
                in a flood of cement,
        poisons left for possum,
                traps left for fox—
                      an assault
        on all of us,
                and watch how fast we spill

our own blood. Oh, Earth
      please hold us,
            enfold us, transform
      us the way the lichens
            transform stone.

Nocturne

for D

Some nights, I lose him
when the music begins to braid
like currents in a river—when
the piccolo begins to float
like a meadowlark over the deep
dark valleys of the tympani,
and the violin transcribes
the bright shimmer of trees
on a hillside at dusk.
He gets caught in the net
of sounds, and cradled there,
swaying, he remembers lying
under the piano while his mother
played Debussy and Haydn,
before she drifted into a world
of her own, holding symphonies
only she would ever hear.

How to Capture a Swarm

Lie down in a field of lavender.

Drizzle honey on your tongue.

Find a tree with low hanging branches; press your body against the trunk.

When the wind blows, lift your arms and wait.

The swarm will appear as the head of a bear; reach inside its mouth.

Stinging you will kill them; resist your beating heart.

They will know you; do not be fooled.

Allow their bodies to seduce your wrists.

You may moan, but no louder than they do.

Open a box, clip the branch.

If you're worthy, they will keep you.

What Gates But These Bodies

And maybe it doesn't matter:
which cathedral's truth.
Maybe what matters is
this body in spaces
and the reading of them:
and light broken
into tremulous columns,
the intensity
of the moss's green
as it softens the arches
of the elm's roots
which coil over and between rocks
on the riverbank,
and the frog's throaty vibrato
pouring like liquid
into you.

Joy

It stalks me, knows
where I am, follows me now,

can see me, a wolf at the edge
of the pine forest watching as I run

through panes of light,
against the air that whispers

through the trees, that wants
to lift me up like a sail.

Nothing scares me more
than being unhinged

but when a dove lands before me
I stop short, caught breathless,

breaking open, torn from the trough
of despair I feel so safe in. No choice

but to rise, and I am stretched out,
devoured, expanding into the trees, this bird,

no *I*, only *we*, untethered to *me*
and instead, inside of everything

mortal and earthbound.

Then

I wake to sleep and take my waking slow . . .
—Theodore Roethke

Pressing against
      this unknown,

this unknowing,
      I am a fallen leaf

against the wall of soil.
      Only by softening

will I enter.
      See how the light

pours through
      the leafless trees?

Only by dissolving
      this mask

of separation,
      by becoming

porous enough
      can we

begin to fill,
      to belong.

Like the hollows
                of the tree filling

with moss, with fungi,
        with breeze.

Field Notes: White Shark

Oh, Big Fish, are you lonely? You
who did not choose your fierce body,
which does as any body does
with the gifts it has been given. Your body
which is blade, carving the dark salt currents
across the unknowable depths where I floated
but did not belong. Your body which is mouth—
rows of ragged teeth, each longer than my thumb
to which nothing will not succumb. How is it
your gills magic oxygen from the substance
that would drown me? I held my breath
when I saw you, my awkward limbs pawing
the blue. Does anyone pause to gaze into your
fathomless indigo eyes? I confess I
looked away. Does your rough gunmetal skin
long to be touched like mine does?
What did you want from me, Big Fish?
I had waited a lifetime for you.
Were you carrying your children
in your belly, like I have done, who would,
after so many months, swim from you,
the way dreams leave our heads when we wake?
Or were you, yourself, a child? Maybe
you were weary? Or wary of my kind?
I have seen what we do to you. The way
we cut you and release you— finless—back
to bleed out in the sea or the way we lure you
with chum and cages, for display, and blame
you when things go awry. I apologize

for the years I let you down, repeating
the story that robbed you. You swam on,
that day, as I did, but I wonder had I stayed . . .?
But, oh Great Fish, I'm a fool. No one
will ever tame you.

When the Time Comes

Dress me in moss. Adorn
my hair with dandelions.
Hum our songs as you
drip water from the spring
over my closed eyes and
cheeks. Carry me through
the maples to the lakeside
where the widest sycamore
leans. Call to the birds then.
Summon the muskrat.
Remember I am with you—
the wind will remind.
Listen for crickets and bees,
my loves, and for my
presence, mycorrhizal.

Gleam

—Lake Edge, January

In the same way ice
    carries light
        by which I mean   *changed, intensified*

        by which I mean kaleidoscopic   *or transformed*
        by which I mean   *a suddenly-*
    visible spectrum   *from violet*
            to cerulean to rose
this body
        by which I mean this
        thorax this spine this skin
    carries awareness.

This being,
    these beings
        by which I mean all,
      by which I mean   *carp antelope lichen*
          and birds   *the lightest of all*
            who live on wind
are allowed to
    bear witness
      to gravity to iron   *to calcium and blood*
        and to the shimmer of rime ice
      to the glint of gold   *on a honeybee wing*
        to the flint
          of a lover's eyes,
        this gleam of late afternoon sun.
And to witness
    also fists and teeth
      breakage and war

so briefly,
       so very briefly
              by which I mean death
                    by which I mean   *you may shine*
       before the end.

Acknowledgments

Thank you to following journals and anthologies for publishing these poems:

Amsterdam Quarterly: "History"

Amethyst: "Joy," "Mortal"

Anti-Heroin Chic: "Field Notes: Cedar Waxwing," "Kermit," "Then"

Becoming Feral: "How to Capture a Swarm"

Catamaran: "Wile E. Coyote"

Dossier Journal: "Poem Which Borrows Its Section Titles from Albums by The Cure"

The Hopper: "Gleam" (as "Lake Edge: January")

MacQueen's Quinterly: "Nocturne," "When the Time Comes"

ONE ART: "On the Day After You Left This World," "Ritual for the New Ancestors"

Terrain: "Crop Duster," "Synapse," "While the World Burned On"

"Invitation" was published in *An Elemental Life,* ed. Gavin Van Horn, Center for Humans and Nature Anthology, 2024.

"On the Day After You Left This World" and "While the World

Burned On" were published in *Poetry of Presence II,* eds. Phyllis Cole Dai and Ruby Wilson, Grayson Books, 2023.

"Metaphor," "Redress for Michelangelo," "What Gates But These Bodies," and "The Words of Noah's Wife" were published in *The Edge of Damage,* a limited edition chapbook (Parallel Press, 2007).

I am grateful for the encouragement and inspiration I encountered as I made these poems. Thank you Jane Hirshfield, Laurie Sheck, Paul, Ginny, and Stephanie Soldner, Ron Wallace, Jesse Lee Kercheval, Judith Claire Mitchell, Amaud Jamaul Johnson, Cherene Sherrard, Gregg Mitman, David Zimmerman, James Crews, J.L. Conrad, J. Drew Lanham, Nickole Brown, Stella Nelson, Catherine Jagoe, Lailah Shima, Nathan Jandl, Gwenola Caradec, Joe Parisi, Lynne Dennis, and Susan Willis. Thank you to my wonderful editor, Diane Lockward, and Terrapin Books for believing in my work. Thank you to my brilliant parents, the late painter, Arthur Kdav, and the potter, Stephanie O'Shaughnessy who showed me that a life of art is difficult, but possible, and so very rewarding. Thank you to my generous sisters: Anna, for sticking by me through everything, and Jenny, for always reminding the world of nature's magic. My days are imbued with the light, love, and laughter brought by my children, Elijah and Maia. Thank you, you two beautiful spirits. And thank you, Drew Szabo, for making such joyful music of this precious life.

About the Author

Heather Swan is the author of the poetry collection *A Kinship with Ash* (Terrapin Books), which was a finalist for the ASLE Book Award, and the chapbook *The Edge of Damage* (Parallel Press), which won the Wisconsin Chapbook Award. She is also the author of the non-fiction book *Where Honeybees Thrive: Stories from the Field* (Penn State Press), which won the Sigurd F. Olson Nature Writing Award, and a companion book, *Where the Grass Still Sings: Stories of Insects and Interconnection.* She is the recipient of an Illinois Arts Council Fellowship, the Maud Weinshenk Award, and the August Derleth Prize for Poetry. She teaches environmental literature and writing at the University of Wisconsin-Madison.